TO AN AMAZING MOM

FROM

Published by Christian Art Publishers
PO Box 1599, Vereeniging, 1930, RSA

© 2019
First edition 2019

Designed by Christian Art Publishers

Images used under license from Shutterstock.com

Printed in China

ISBN 978-1-4321-2994-1

19 20 21 22 23 24 25 26 27 28 – 12 11 10 9 8 7 6 5 4 3

LIFE LISTS
FOR
Mothers

**CHRISTIAN ART
PUBLISHERS**

FOR *everything* THERE IS A season, a time FOR EVERY activity under *heaven.*

ECCLESIASTES 3:1

10 WAYS TO *love*

1 Listen without interrupting.
Proverbs 18:13

2 Speak without accusing.
James 1:19

3 Give without sparing.
Proverbs 21:26

4 Pray without ceasing.
1 Thessalonians 5:17

5 Answer without arguing.
Proverbs 17:1

6 Love without pretending.

Romans 12:9-10

7 Enjoy without complaining.

Philippians 2:14

8 Trust without wavering.

1 Corinthians 13:7

9 Forgive without punishing.

Colossians 3:13

10 Promise without forgetting.

Luke 16:10

6 LESSONS
FROM
Galatians

1. Don't live for the approval of others.

   GALATIANS 1:10

2. You are not defined by your past.

   GALATIANS 2:20

3. Your worth is in Christ, not in your job or education.

   GALATIANS 6:14

4. You are no longer a slave,
   you are now a child of God.

   GALATIANS 4:7

5. Don't be led by feelings and emotions,
   be led by the Spirit.

   GALATIANS 5:17-19

6. Don't grow weary while doing good.
   When the time is right, you will reap
   what you've sown.

   GALATIANS 6:9

BEFORE YOU SPEAK
THINK

T = IS IT TRUE?

H = IS IT HELPFUL?

I = IS IT INSPIRING?

N = IS IT NECESSARY?

K = IS IT KIND?

WHEN SHE SPEAKS,
HER WORDS ARE WISE,
AND SHE GIVES
INSTRUCTIONS WITH
KINDNESS.

PROVERBS 31:26

MAY THE *God* OF HOPE
FILL *you* WITH ALL
JOY &
peace AS
you trust
IN HIM.

ROMANS 15:13

What are your dreams
and hopes for your children?

IN OUR
home we...

Are always honest.
Proverbs 12:22

Forgive and forget.
Proverbs 17:9

Are kindhearted.
Ephesians 4:32

Work hard.
Colossians 3:23

Are thankful.
1 Thessalonians 5:18

Never give up.
Philippians 4:13

Love one another.
1 Peter 1:22

Thank God for our blessings.
Ephesians 1:3

Encourage each other.
1 Thessalonians 4:18

As for
ME AND MY
HOUSE,
WE WILL SERVE
THE
Lord.

Joshua 24:15

WRITE DOWN 7 THINGS YOU ARE

grateful

FOR TODAY:

1

2

3

4

5

6

7

Give thanks
TO THE LORD,
FOR HE IS good;
HIS
love ENDURES
forever.

PSALM 107:1

Nine Prayers
TO PRAY DAILY FOR YOUR CHILDREN

1. Salvation
2. Conviction of Sin
3. Love for God's Word
4. Protection from evil
5. Wisdom and discernment
6. Godly friendships
7. Obedience to God's will
8. Courage to stand firm in their faith
9. Joy in the Lord

FIX THESE WORDS OF MINE
IN YOUR *hearts* & MINDS.
TEACH
THEM TO YOUR CHILDREN,
talking ABOUT THEM WHEN YOU
SIT AT HOME
AND WHEN YOU
WALK ALONG THE ROAD,
WHEN YOU LIE DOWN
AND WHEN YOU *get up.*

YOU knit me
TOGETHER IN MY
mother's WOMB.

List 10 things you love about each of your
children that makes them unique:

[1]

[2]

[3]

[4]

[5]

I *praise* YOU BECAUSE I AM fearfully AND *wonderfully* MADE.

PSALM 139:13-14

[6]

[7]

[8]

[9]

[10]

9 WAYS TO LIVE A MORE

positive life

STOP...

- playing the victim
- making excuses
- letting society tell you how to live
- relying on others to make you happy
- doubting yourself
- trying to make other people happy

LIVE A *life* FILLED WITH *love.*

START...

- positive thinking
- believing in yourself
- turning off gadgets and spending time outside
- expressing your creativity
- acknowledging your dreams and wishes
- finding joy in God alone

FOLLOWING THE EXAMPLE OF *Christ.*
EPHESIANS 5:2

List your favorite Scripture verses
to pray over your family.

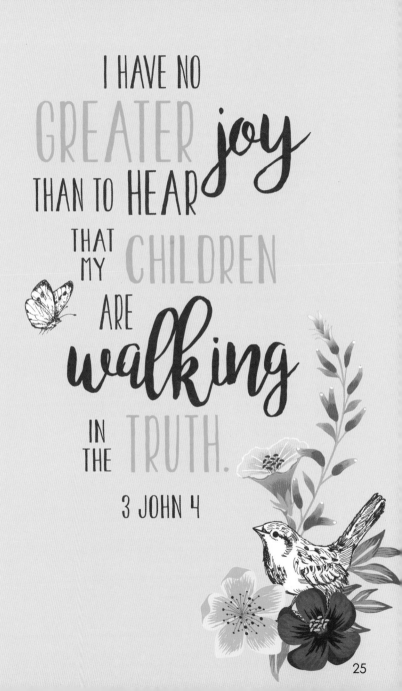

I HAVE NO
GREATER *joy*
THAN TO HEAR
THAT MY CHILDREN
ARE
walking
IN THE TRUTH.

3 JOHN 4

WAITING
FOR GOD MEANS

YOU'RE ALLOWING HIM TO DO
WHAT HE DOES BEST ...

Watch god work in his way

Ask god about his purposes

Invite god to work in your heart

Trust god to fulfill his plans for you

WAIT PATIENTLY
FOR THE *Lord.*

Psalm 27:14

Today's
TO-DO LIST

1 PRAY ABOUT EVERYTHING

2 WORRY ABOUT NOTHING

3 PRAISE LAVISHLY

4 CRITICIZE SPARINGLY

5 GIVE GENEROUSLY

6 FORGIVE COMPLETELY

7 LOVE UNCONDITIONALLY

THIS IS THE DAY
THAT THE LORD HAS MADE.
LET US *rejoice*
AND BE GLAD
TODAY!

PSALM 118:24

9 THINGS TO TELL YOUR *Child* OFTEN

[1] You make me proud.
[2] I love being your mom!
[3] I believe in you.
[4] You don't have to be perfect to be great.
[5] You are important and loved.

[6] I know you did your best.
[7] Seeing you happy makes me happy.
[8] I forgive you.
[9] You make my heart smile.

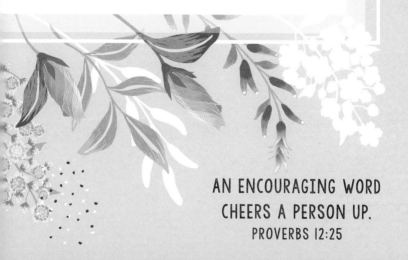

AN ENCOURAGING WORD
CHEERS A PERSON UP.
PROVERBS 12:25

A
HAPPY
HEART
MAKES THE FACE
cheerful.

PROVERBS 15:13

LIST 3 THINGS
THAT MADE YOU *smile*
TODAY

1

2

3

EIGHT WAYS
TO CARE FOR YOUR CHILDREN

ONE PRAY FOR THEM

TWO SMILE

THREE FORGIVE

FOUR SPEAK KINDNESS

FIVE HUG THEM

SIX LOOK THEM IN THE EYES

SEVEN MOTIVATE THEM

EIGHT LOVE THEM

ENCOURAGE
ONE ANOTHER
& BUILD
EACH OTHER UP.

1 THESSALONIANS 5:11

8 BIBLE VERSES
TO HOLD ON TO *today*

Wisdom If you need wisdom,
ask our generous God, and He will give it to you.
JAMES 1:5

Thoughts
Guard your heart above all else, for it
determines the course of your life.

PROVERBS 4:23

Worry

Don't worry about anything; instead,
pray about everything. **PHILIPPIANS 4:6**

Anger
You must all be quick to listen,
slow to speak, and slow to get angry.

JAMES 1:19

Truth The LORD delights
in people who are trustworthy.
PROVERBS 12:22

Conduct

Let everything you say be good and helpful,
so that your words will be an encouragement
to those who hear them.

EPHESIANS 4:29

Love is patient, love is kind.
It always protects, always trusts,
always hopes, always perseveres.

1 CORINTHIANS 13:4, 7

Kindness

Be kind and compassionate to one another,
forgiving each other,
just as in Christ God forgave you.

EPHESIANS 4:32

7 RULES FOR A LIFE OF

abundance

1 Make peace with your past so it won't disturb your present.

2 Don't worry about what others think of you.

3 Time heals almost everything. Give it time.

4 Choose joy.

5 Don't compare your life to others'.

6 Don't judge others, you don't know their journey.

7 Stop thinking too much. It's all right not to know the answers.

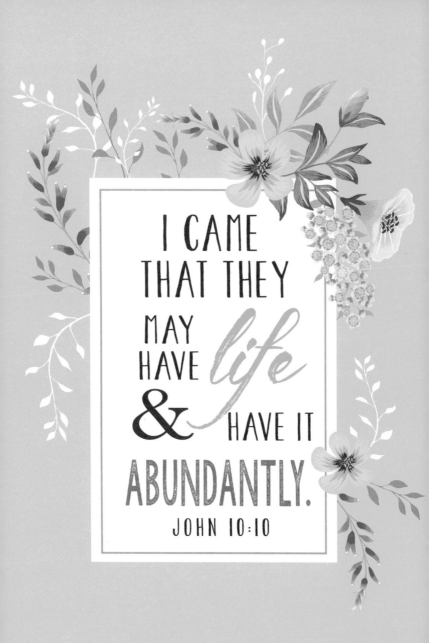

I CAME
THAT THEY
MAY *life*
HAVE
& HAVE IT
ABUNDANTLY.
JOHN 10:10

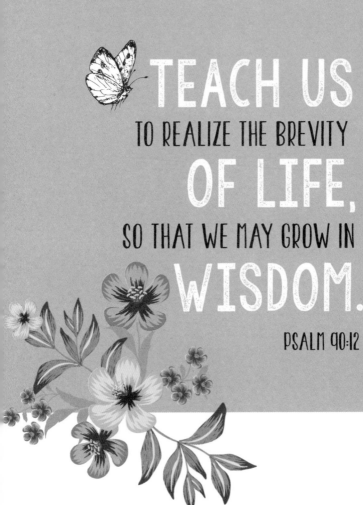

TEACH US TO REALIZE THE BREVITY **OF LIFE,** SO THAT WE MAY GROW IN **WISDOM.**

PSALM 90:12

KEEP IT SIMPLE

LET IT GO

TELL THE TRUTH

LEARN FROM OTHERS

UNSUBSCRIBE

SAY I'M SORRY

BE HONEST WITH YOURSELF

AVOID THE DRAMA

LEARN FROM YOUR MISTAKES

THINK BEFORE YOU SPEAK

PRIORITIZE

5 RULES FOR LIVING AN EXTRAORDINARY *life*

[1] Free your heart
from hatred

[2] Free your mind
from worries

[3] Live simply

[4] Give more

[5] Expect less

"Give and you
will receive.

Your gift will return to you in full -
pressed down, shaken together
to make room for more, running over,
and poured into your lap.
The amount you give will determine
the amount you get back."

Luke 6:38

TODAY...

love

inspire

listen

teach

motivate

laugh

6 TIPS FOR A GOOD *life*

BEFORE
YOU WORRY
pray

1

BEFORE
YOU SPEAK
listen

2

3

BEFORE
YOU WRITE
think

6 BEFORE YOU DIE *live*

5 BEFORE YOU QUIT *try*

4 BEFORE YOU SPEND *earn*

Nurture HOPE & JOY
in your family

ALWAYS BE HUMBLE

& *gentle*

BE PATIENT

making allowance for each

KEEP YOURSELVES UNITED

IN THE *Spirit,*

BINDING

[1] Pray for them
[2] Serve them
[3] Encourage them
[4] Love them

WITH EACH OTHER,

ther's faults
because of your *love.*

YOURSELVES *together*
WITH PEACE. EPHESIANS 4:2-3

YOU ARE CLOTHED WITH ...

SALVATION
Isaiah 61:10

Grace
2 Corinthians 9:13-15

Joy
Psalm 30:11

POWER
Luke 24:49

Love
1 John 3:1

RIGHTEOUSNESS
Isaiah 32:17

PROTECTION
Psalm 5:11

Peace
Colossians 3:15

51

Five PRAYERS
TO PRAY FOR YOUR CHILDREN DAILY

1. That they would choose to follow Jesus.

2. That their thoughts would be pure.

3. That they would choose friends wisely.

4. That they would have the courage to do what's right.

5. That they would make a difference in this world.

Heavenly Father,

I won't give up on parenting
my kids because You never give
up on me. Sustain me when
I feel I don't have what it takes.
I look to You for the wisdom
I need in any moment.
Teach me to live in step
with You so that Your resources
are always at my disposal.

Amen.

LESS IS MORE

LESS	MORE
TALKING	LISTENING
PLANNING	ENCOURAGING
COMPLAINING	SMILING
WORRYING	UNDERSTANDING
DOUBTING	WORKING OUT
FROWNING	GRATITUDE

You
make known to me
the path of life;
You will fill me with joy in Your presence,
with eternal pleasures at
Your right hand.

Psalm 16:11

5 *Questions* YOU SHOULD ASK YOURSELF OFTEN

1 Who makes you happy, and why?

2 Which things on your daily schedule are helping you to fulfill your godly purpose?

3 What qualities and talents come naturally to you?

4 What life lesson or insight have you gained from a recent struggle?

5 What's on your to-do list that doesn't need to be?

YOU CAN
MAKE MANY
plans,
BUT THE
LORD'S
purpose
WILL PREVAIL.

PROVERBS 19:21

57

27

9 KEYS
FOR A FAITH-FILLED *family*

1. Count your blessings.
   Psalm 100

2. Bear each other's burdens.
   Galatians 6:2

3. Be kind and tenderhearted.
   Ephesians 4:32

4. Comfort one another.
   1 Thessalonians 4:18

5. Keep your promises.
   Matthew 5:37

6. Be supportive of one another.
   Acts 20:35

7. Be true to each other.
   Revelation 15:3

8. Look after each other.
   Deuteronomy 15:11

9. Treat each other well.
   Matthew 7:12

L♥VE

ONE ANOTHER
DEEPLY, FROM THE

heart.

I PETER 1:22

4 Ways
TO BE A
Godly Mother

1. Speak life

2. Build up

3. Help others

4. Spread grace

DO NOT
LET ANY
UNWHOLESOME TALK

come out of your mouths,
but only what is

helpful

FOR building

others up.

EPHESIANS 4:29

THE JOURNEY OF *healing* IS ONE OF ACTION ...

1 LET GO

GOD MENDS ME

START OVER 2

GOD MOLDS ME

MOVE AHEAD 3

GOD MATURES ME

"I AM THE LORD WHO *heals* YOU."

EXODUS 15:26

A *Mom's*
STRESS-RELIEF GUIDE

[1] Renew your mind. Romans 12:2

[2] Persevere. James 1:2-4

[3] Seek peace. John 14:27

[4] Accept grace. Romans 16:20

[5] Commit to the Lord. Proverbs 16:3

[6] Give your cares to Him. Matthew 11:28-30

[7] He'll take care of you. Psalm 55:22

[8] Soar on wings like eagles. Isaiah 40:31

[9] Keep your eyes on Him. Psalm 16:8

[10] God's plans are for good. Jeremiah 29:11

31

A PLEDGE
TO
love yourself

I WILL
- ♥ forgive myself for the mistakes I make
- ♥ love my body just the way it is
- ♥ accept that I am not perfect
- ♥ never talk down to myself
- ♥ never let my fears and doubts hold me back
- ♥ not worry too much what others think of me
- ♥ honor my dreams
- ♥ be thankful for my life
- ♥ be understanding, patient and kind to myself
- ♥ have fun!

For we are
God's masterpiece.
He has
created us anew in

CHRIST JESUS,

so we can do the

good things
HE

PLANNED FOR US

long ago.

Ephesians 2:10

32

5 DAYS TO AN ATTITUDE OF *Gratitude*

DAY 1   List 5 things you're grateful for today.

DAY 2   Which two things do you value most about yourself?

DAY 3   List 3 things that made you smile today

DAY 4   Recall a time when God answered your prayer.

DAY 5   Recall one of the happiest moments in your life?

LET THE
message
ABOUT
Christ,
IN ALL ITS
RICHNESS,
fill YOUR LIVES.

COLOSSIANS 3:16

3 TIPS

FOR MEMORIZING

SCRIPTURE VERSES

1 READ IT 10 TIMES

2 SPEAK IT 10 TIMES

3 WRITE IT 2 TIMES

14 ESSENTIALS
FOR A
Balanced LIFE

1. **LEAVE WORK** at work
2. **LET GO** and let God
3. Always tell the **TRUTH**
4. **LISTEN** attentively
5. It's OK to **ASK FOR HELP**
6. **NO** is also an answer
7. **DECLUTTER** your life

8. **LEARN** from others
9. **LEAVE THE PAST** in the past
10. Never be too proud to **APOLOGIZE**
11. **APPRECIATE** the little things
12. Be **CONTENT** with what you have
13. **PLAN** for an emergency
14. Establish clear **BOUNDARIES**

Don't you realize that your
body is the temple of the Holy Spirit?
So you must honor God with your body.

1 Corinthians 6: 19-20

35

6 Great Reasons
TO PRAY

First we pray because we are God's children and He loves to hear from us! Zephaniah 3:17

Second we pray because it deepens our trust in God. Philippians 4:6-7

Third we pray because it causes us to depend on God. Isaiah 40:26

Fourth, we pray because it gives us the chance to express ourselves completely to the Lord. Psalm 62:8

Fifth, we pray because our prayers move the heart of God. James 4:2

Sixth, we pray because it's an amazing way to get involved with what God is already doing in our world.

1 Thessalonians 5:25

God shapes the world by prayer. The more praying there is in the world, the better the world will be, the mightier the forces against evil.

Mother Teresa

36

A 7-DAY CHALLENGE
TO BE MORE

thankful

ENTER HIS GATES
WITH THANKSGIVING;
GO INTO HIS COURTS
WITH PRAISE.
GIVE THANKS TO HIM
AND PRAISE HIS NAME.
HIS UNFAILING LOVE
CONTINUES FOREVER,
AND HIS FAITHFULNESS
CONTINUES TO EACH
GENERATION.

PSALM 100:4-5

1. Write down the blessings that you've experienced today.

   ----

2. Which relationships in your life make you feel blessed?

   ----

3. Write down your favorite affirmations.

   ----

4. How can you inject gratitude into a current situation?

   ----

5. Which fears have you overcome?

   ----

6. What everyday items are you most grateful for?

   ----

7. Describe the last time your heart was overflowing with joy.

She WHO KNEELS BEFORE God CAN STAND BEFORE ANYONE.

"If you believe, you will receive whatever you ask for in prayer."

Matthew 21:22

Moms

WHO PRAY SHOULD ...

POUR OUT THEIR HEARTS

ALWAYS BELIEVE

YIELD TO WHAT GOD TELLS THEM

REALIZE THAT GOD WILL ANSWER

7 MATTERS OF THE HEART FOR *Mothers*

1 - PRAYER

2 - LOVE

3 - COMPASSION

4 - FORGIVENESS

5 - GRATITUDE

6 - JOY

7 - INTEGRITY

I pray that your hearts will be flooded with light so that you can understand the confident hope He has given to those He called.

Ephesians 1:18

Love the Lord above all else.

1 Corinthians 7:35

40

Bible VIRTUES

Self-control
1 THESS. 5:6

Salvation
2 TIM. 2:10

INTEGRITY AND honesty
PS. 25:21

God,
let my children
be alert and able
to control their
emotions. Grant
them a pure spirit.
Amen.

Lord,
I pray for the
salvation of my
children, that they
will choose Jesus,
and bring glory
to His name.
Amen.

Lord Jesus,
I pray that
integrity will be
planted in the hearts
of my children as
they put their
hope in You.
Amen.

Children

Courage
DEUT. 31:6

Kindness
I THESS. 5:15

Mercy
LUKE 6:36

God, I want my children to know that You will never leave them. They can have courage because You are their God. Amen.

Lord Jesus, create a kind and pure spirit in the hearts of my children, so that they will always put others before themselves. Amen.

God, instill in my children compassion and mercy for others. Let them follow in Your steps always. Amen.

41

The joy OF THE *Lord* IS YOUR strength.

NEHEMIAH 8:10

8 THINGS TO DO
FOR A
JOY-FILLED DAY

\# WATCH A SUNRISE

\# BUY A BUNCH OF FRESH FLOWERS

\# GO FOR A WALK AND ENJOY CREATION

\# GIVE SOMEONE YOU LOVE A BEAR HUG

\# PLAY WITH YOUR CHILDREN

\# PUT ON MUSIC AND DANCE

\# MEET A FRIEND FOR COFFEE

\# READ AN INSPIRATIONAL BOOK.

4 LISTS
TO MAKE WHEN LIFE SEEMS HARD

1 Things that inspire you:

- -

- -

- -

- -

2 Things you love about yourself:

- -

- -

- -

- -

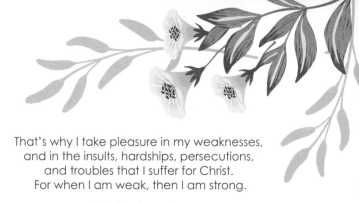

That's why I take pleasure in my weaknesses,
and in the insults, hardships, persecutions,
and troubles that I suffer for Christ.
For when I am weak, then I am strong.

2 Corinthians 12:10

3 Your happiest memories so far:

_____

_____

_____

_____

4 Your favorite people and why:

_____

_____

_____

_____

43

Love
THE LORD
YOUR GOD
WITH ALL YOUR
HEART
AND WITH ALL YOUR
SOUL
AND WITH ALL YOUR
STRENGTH.
LUKE 10:27

7 HEALTHY HABITS
FOR EVERY *Mom*

1 MAKE PEACE WITH WHO YOU ARE

2 HAVE REGULAR QUIET TIMES

3 CELEBRATE EVERYDAY SUCCESSES

4 TAKE FIVE DEEP BREATHS BEFORE YOU EAT

5 PRIORITIZE SELF-CARE AND FUN

6 STOP CRITICIZING YOURSELF

7 SEEK SUPPORT AND POSITIVE MENTORS

A 6-Day Challenge

DAY 1 A good deed I'm going to do today:

DAY 2 I'm going to learn this new skill:

DAY 3 A book I'd like to read:

DAY 4 A new food I'm going to try:

DAY 5 I'm going to do better today at:

DAY 6 I'm going to break the following habit:

God has made everything beautiful for its own time.

ECCLESIASTES 3:11

5 Scriptures FOR MAKING good DECISIONS

1 Tune out distractions
— Luke 5:16

2 Seek advice from good friends
— Proverbs 19:20

3 Ask God for wisdom
— James 1:5

4 Let God direct you
— Proverbs 16:9

5 Give thanks for the answers
— Psalm 28:7

6 STEPS TO BECOME A
Wiser Mom

1. Fear the Lord

2. Study the Bible

3. Seek godly counsel when needed

4. Listen to the Holy Spirit

5. Trust the Lord

6. Speak with kindness.

COME AND LISTEN
TO MY COUNSEL.
I'LL SHARE MY HEART
WITH YOU AND
MAKE YOU WISE.

PROVERBS 1:23

20 REASONS TO *praise God*

GOD ...

1 is a personal God

2 is the Sovereign King

3 is GREAT

4 is unsearchable

5 acts on my behalf

6 is majestic

7 is good

8 is righteous

9 is gracious

10 is full of compassion

11   is slow to anger

12   is merciful

13   is powerful

14   makes Himself known to me

15   helps me

16   provides for me

17   is generous

18   is near to me

19   preserves me

20   brings justice to my life.

Every day I will praise Your name. Psalm 145:2

48

BE LOVE

HAVE	LOVE
GIVE	LOVE
RECEIVE	LOVE
EMBRACE	LOVE
ALWAYS	LOVE

LOVE

is patient,
love is kind ...

It does not dishonor others,
it is not self-seeking, it is not easily
angered, it keeps no record
of wrongs ... It always protects,
always trusts, always hopes,
always perseveres.

1 Corinthians
13:4-5, 7

Mom, REMEMBER:

PSALM 25:5
AT YOUR LOWEST ...

PSALM 27:1
AT YOUR DARKEST ...

PSALM 118:14
AT YOUR WEAKEST ...

ISAIAH 66:13
AT YOUR SADDEST ...

GOD IS YOUR *hope*

GOD IS YOUR *light*

GOD IS YOUR *strength*

GOD IS YOUR *comforter*

A LASTING TO-DO *list* FOR *Moms*

1 SMILE WITHOUT HESITATING

GIVE WITHOUT EXPECTING **2**

3 NOTICE WITHOUT CRITIQUING

GUIDE WITHOUT PUSHING **4**

5 FORGIVE WITHOUT RESENTING

LAUGH WITHOUT MOCKING **6**

7 APPRECIATE WITHOUT COMPARING

LOVE WITH ALL YOUR HEART! **8**

"WHERE YOUR *treasure* IS, THERE YOUR *heart* WILL BE ALSO."

MATTHEW 6:21

51

As you study the

GREET ➡

READ ➡

OBSERVE ➡

WRITE ➡

Invite God into your quiet time by opening in prayer.

Read the verse silently or out loud a few times.

What stood out for you as you read this verse?

Write out the verse, your observations and a prayer.

They delight in the law of the LORD, meditating on it day and night.
Psalm 1:2

10 WAYS TO PLEASE God

1 Do the right things
for the right reasons.
Matthew 6:1-8

2 Pray God's
agenda,
not yours.
Matthew 6:9-13

3 Forgive others.
Matthew 6:14-15

4 Prioritize eternal things,
not temporal ones.
Matthew 6:19-24

5 Do not worry.
Matthew 6:25-31

6 Seek the Kingdom first.
Matthew 6:33-34

7 Do not judge others.
Matthew 7:1-5

8 Do to others as you would have done to you.
Matthew 7:12

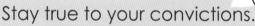
9 Stay true to your convictions.
Matthew 7:13-20

10 Obey God.
Matthew 7:21-27

53

RAISING
YOUR CHILDREN GOD'S WAY

ONE

In every matter consider your child's heart.

Above all else,
guard your heart,
for everything you
do flows from it.

PROVERBS 4:23

FIVE

Listen to Him.

"My sheep listen to My voice;
I know them, and they follow Me."

JOHN 10:27

FOUR

Worship God with all your heart.

Everything on earth will worship You;
they will sing Your praises, shouting
Your name in glorious songs.

PSALM 66:4

TWO

Pray with your children.

He told them a parable
to the effect that they ought
always to pray and not lose heart.

LUKE 18:1

THREE

Study the Bible with
your children.

I rejoiced greatly to find
some of your children
walking in the truth.

2 JOHN 4

54

PRAYING
THE ACTS
way

1 **A**doration
Praising the Lord

2 **C**onfession
Admit your sins

3 **T**hanksgiving
Thanking God

4 **S**upplication
Praying for loved ones

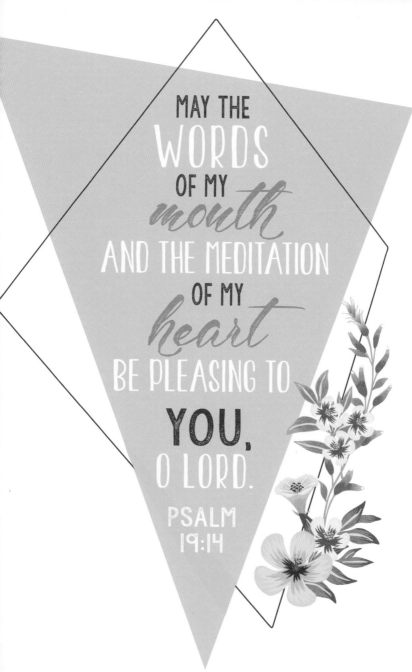

MAY THE
WORDS
OF MY
mouth
AND THE MEDITATION
OF MY
heart
BE PLEASING TO
YOU,
O LORD.
PSALM
19:14

55

5 Tips FOR STAYING focused ON GOD THROUGHOUT THE day

1 Start your day with Him, reading His Word and praying.

2 When you catch yourself getting distracted, refocus on Him.

3 Measure yourself against God's Word and remove sin from your life.

4 Talk to Him throughout your day, even if it is just a quick prayer.

5 End off your day with Him, reading His Word and praying.

Set your minds on things above, not on earthly things.
Colossians 3:2

56

HOW TO BE A
Godly MOM

♡ Spend time meditating on God's Word.

♡ Choose joy every day.

♡ Be a prayer warrior.

♡ Make others feel special.

♡ Be considerate and kind.

♡ Let God's light shine through you.

♡ Do everything in love.

♡ Make God your first priority.

"Let your light shine before others,
that they may see your good deeds
and glorify your Father in heaven."

Matthew 5:16

6 THINGS
YOU SHOULD
ALWAYS DO

Work hard.

[1]

Colossians 3:23

Keep your promises.

[2]

Luke 16:10

[3] Tell the truth.

Proverbs 12:22

[4] Count your blessings.

Psalm 34:1-3

[5] Love one another.

1 Peter 1:22

[6] Have FUN!

Proverbs 15:13

Love each other deeply with all your heart.
1 PETER 1:22

58

Fix YOUR
thoughts
ON WHAT IS *true*
& HONORABLE,
AND right,
AND PURE
& *lovely,*
AND
admirable.
PHILIPPIANS 4:8

PRAYERS FOR A
Mom's Heart

Lord,
Help me to love You first, with all my heart, mind and soul. Matthew 22:37

Amen

Lord,
Help me to learn to be content with whatever the circumstance. Philippians 4:11-12

Amen

Lord,
Let me put away all bitterness, and be kind, tenderhearted, and forgiving as Christ forgave me. Ephesians 4:31-32

Amen

Lord,
Let me always remember that Your grace is sufficient for me. 2 Corinthians 12:9

Amen

59

3 WAYS
TO GUARD AGAINST
Temptation

1. Jesus told him, "No! The Scriptures say, 'People do not live by bread alone, but by every word that comes from the mouth of God.'" MATTHEW 4:4

2. Jesus said to him, "It is written again, 'You shall not tempt the LORD your God.'" MATTHEW 4:7

3. Jesus said to him, "Away from Me, Satan! For it is written: 'Worship the Lord your God, and serve Him only.'" MATTHEW 4:10

SOS

GOD IS
faithful;
HE
WILL NOT
LET YOU BE TEMPTED BEYOND
WHAT YOU CAN BEAR.
I CORINTHIANS 10:13

60

Scriptures to help YOU STAND STRONG

KEEP ALERT.
BE FIRM IN YOUR
FAITH,
STAY BRAVE
& STRONG.

1 CORINTHIANS 16:13

I CORINTHIANS 10:13

The temptations in your life are no different from what others experience. And God is faithful. He will not allow the temptation to be more than you can stand. When you are tempted, He will show you a way out so that you can endure.

JAMES 1:12

God blesses those who patiently endure testing and temptation. Afterward they will receive the crown of life that God has promised to those who love Him.

HEBREWS 2:18

Because He Himself suffered when He was tempted, He is able to help those who are being tempted.

61

10 PRAYERS throughout the day

9 MINUTES of Scripture meditation

8 HOURS of sleep

7 THOUSAND steps daily, preferably in nature

6 HEALTHY, small meals

Don't you realize that your body is the temple of the Holy Spirit? So you must honor God with your body.

1 Corinthians 6:19-20

10 STEPS TO AN ABUNDANT *life*

1 HOUR of being active

2 LITERS of water

3 CUPS of your favorite coffee or tea

4 SHORT mental breaks per day

5 MINUTES of laughter

62

MEDITATE ON HIS *Words*

The SOAP Method

S CRIPTURE

O BSERVATION

A PPLICATION

P RAYER

Write out a verse that was meaningful to you.

What did you learn?
What was God saying to you?

How can you apply the Scripture to
your life and let it change you?

Respond to God, praying and using
Scripture as your guide. Ask God to
help you apply Scripture to your life.

Blessed is the one whose delight
is in the law of the LORD, and who meditates
on His law day and night.

Psalm 1:1-2

63

Guide me
IN YOUR TRUTH
& *teach* ME,
FOR YOU ARE GOD
my Savior
& MY HOPE
IS IN YOU.

PSALM 25:5

6 REASONS TO READ THE *Bible*

1. To get rid of anxiety and have peace.

Psalm 119:165

2. To experience healing and deliverance.

Psalm 107:20

3. To know what's really in your heart.

Hebrews 4:12

4. To have direction and know God's will.

Psalm 119:105

5. To have strength, comfort and hope.

Psalm 119:28, 50, 114

6. To build faith.

Romans 10:17

131

64

5 KINDS OF WOMEN

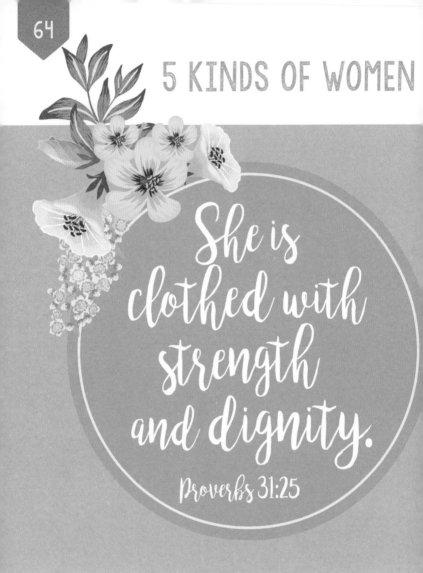

She is clothed with strength and dignity.

Proverbs 31:25

THE *world* NEEDS

The world has enough women who are tough;
we need women who are ... *tender.*

There are enough women who are coarse;
we need women who are ... *kind.*

There are enough women of fame and fortune;
we need women of ... *faith.*

We have enough greed;
we need more ... *goodness.*

We have enough popularity;
we need ... *purity.*

65

Exodus 20

THE TEN COMMANDS FOR MOMS

1 Love God more than anything else.

2 Worship only God.

3 Always respect God's name.

4 Rest on the seventh day and honor the Lord.

5 Honor your father and mother.

Don't hurt anyone.

Be true to your spouse.

Don't take things that don't belong to you.

Never tell a lie.

Be happy with what you have!

6 7 8 9 10

" If you *love* Me,
         obey My commandments.
    And I will *ask* the Father,
         and He will *give* you another Advocate,
    who will never leave you.
         He is the *Holy Spirit*. "

JOHN 14:15-17

135

66

FROM HIS ABUNDANCE WE HAVE ALL RECEIVED ONE *gracious* BLESSING AFTER ANOTHER.

JOHN 1:16

5 WAYS
TO PRAY FOR YOUR *family*

1. Pray for LOVE.

I pray that our family would love with patience and kindness.

2. Pray for HUMILITY.

I pray that our family would not envy or boast or clothe ourselves with pride.

3. Pray for FORGIVENESS.

I pray that we would keep no record of wrongs and that we would rejoice with the truth.

4. Pray for BALANCE.

I pray that our family will love others as we love ourselves, and that we will respect each other.

5. Pray for FAITH.

I pray that our family would live our lives in Christ, rooted and built up in Him, strengthened in faith, and overflowing with thankfulness.

67

DO what is
love right,
mercy,
& walk
humbly
with your
GOD.

Micah 6:8

10 STEPS to WALK DAILY in HUMILITY

1 Trust God's plans over your own.

2 Always see the best in others.

3 Look for ways to serve others and honor God.

4 Always be courteous and delicate in even difficult situations.

5 Accept insults and injuries as part of life.

6 Ignore your pride and Satan's lies.

7 Do not dwell on the faults of others.

8 Accept small limitations with good humor.

9 Keep busy with your own affairs and not those of others.

10 Speak as little as possible about yourself.

68

Life **IS** *short...*

- 🖤 Choose to enjoy the little things.
- 🖤 Worry less, laugh more.
- 🖤 Let go of fear and anger.
- 🖤 Dance like no one is watching.
- 🖤 Take a deep breath.
- 🖤 Look up at the stars.
- 🖤 Hug your loved ones often.
- 🖤 Sing at the top of your voice.
- 🖤 Love life, go and embrace it.

Make
THE MOST OF
every
opportunity.
EPHESIANS 5:16

Let everything
you say be
good & helpful,
so that your words
will be an
encouragement
to those who hear them.

Ephesians 4:29

6 STEPS TO BEING A *good* MOTHER-IN-LAW

1. Be honest and be yourself.
2. Be considerate of the couple's rights, and don't impose on them.
3. Be sure to treat all partners equally.
4. Be careful not to criticize the one partner to the other.
5. Be careful not to be intrusive or give unsolicited advice.
6. Be sure your attitude is controlled by the Holy Spirit.

70

8 WAYS TO BOOST YOUR
self-esteem

[1] Accept yourself as created in God's image

[2] Anticipate the life God has planned for you

[3] Write down your basic life goals.

[4] Be positive.

[5] Accept God's forgiveness.

[6] Seek first the kingdom of God.

[7] Serve others as God has commanded.

[8] Give thanks in everything.

God created mankind
in His own image.
Genesis 1:27

REMEMBER THE
FRUIT OF THE
spirit

LOVE
compassion for others

JOY
inner gladness that is not
dependent on circumstance.

PEACE
inner contentment

PATIENCE
patient endurance and
perseverance

KINDNESS
thoughtfulness towards others
without seeking reward

GOODNESS
a search for righteousness

FAITHFULNESS
a commitment to God,
spouse, duty

GENTLENESS
consideration for the feelings
of others

SELF-CONTROL
inner strength to control your
emotional, mental and physical
weaknesses

The Holy Spirit produces this kind of fruit
in our lives: love, joy, peace, patience,
kindness, goodness, faithfulness,
gentleness, and self-control.

Galatians 5:22-23

72

16 TRUTHS ABOUT *love*

⟨1⟩ Love is patient

⟨2⟩ Love is kind

⟨3⟩ Love does not envy

⟨4⟩ Love does not boast

⟨5⟩ Love is not proud

⟨6⟩ Love is not rude

⟨7⟩ Love is not self-seeking

⟨8⟩ Love is not easily angered

1 Corinthians 13:4-8

⟨9⟩ Love keeps no record of wrongs

⟨10⟩ Love does not delight in evil

⟨11⟩ Love rejoices with the truth

⟨12⟩ Love always protects

⟨13⟩ Love always trusts

⟨14⟩ Love always hopes

⟨15⟩ Love always perseveres

⟨16⟩ Love never fails

73

3 Results of a
SPIRIT-FILLED LIFE

1. JOYOUS HEART
2. THANKFUL SPIRIT
3. SUBMISSIVE ATTITUDE

Be filled with the Spirit.
Sing and make music
from your heart to the Lord,
always giving thanks to God.

Ephesians 5:18-20

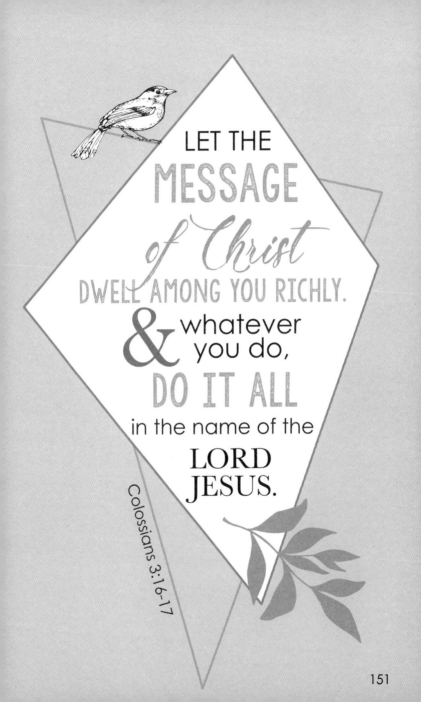

LET THE
MESSAGE
of Christ
DWELL AMONG YOU RICHLY.
& whatever
you do,
DO IT ALL
in the name of the
LORD
JESUS.

Colossians 3:16-17

151

74

5 MINDFUL MOMENTS FOR EVERY Mom

1 In the happy moments, **praise God.**

2 In the difficult moments, **seek God.**

3 In the quiet moments, **worship God.**

4 In the painful moments, **trust God.**

5 Every moment, **thank God.**

DRAW NEAR to **God** and HE WILL DRAW NEAR TO **you.**

James 4:8

6 TRAITS OF A PROVERBS 31 Woman

1 Noble

A wife of noble character who can find? She is worth far more than rubies.

Proverbs 31:10

2 Trustworthy

Her husband can trust her,
and she will greatly enrich his life.
She brings him good, not harm,
all the days of her life.

Proverbs 31:11-12

3 Caring

She rises while it is yet night and provides food for her household.

Proverbs 31:15

4 Diligent

She sets about her work
vigorously; her arms are
strong for her tasks.

Proverbs 31:17

5 Generous

She extends her hand
to the poor, yes, she reaches
out her hands to the needy.

Proverbs 31:20

6 Strong

She is clothed with strength
and dignity, and she laughs
without fear of the future.

Proverbs 31:25

76

5 PIECES OF ADVICE YOU WOULD GIVE TO YOUR *children:*

1. _____

_____

_____

2. _____

_____

_____

3. _____

_____

_____

4. _____

_____

_____

5. _____

_____

_____

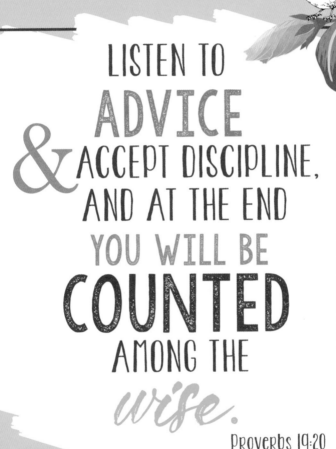

LISTEN TO
ADVICE
& ACCEPT DISCIPLINE,
AND AT THE END
YOU WILL BE
COUNTED
AMONG THE
wise.

Proverbs 19:20

77

4 Reassurances
FOR AN OVERWHELMI[NG]

GOD WILL GIVE YOU REST.
"Come to Me, all of you who are weary and carry heavy burdens, and I will give you rest." Matthew 11:28

GOD IS IN CONTROL.
"Do not fear, for I am with you. I will strengthen you and help you; I will uphold you with My righteous right hand." Isaiah 41:10

GOD WILL CALM THE STORM.

Jesus rebuked the wind and said to the waves, "Silence! Be still!" Suddenly the wind stopped, and there was a great calm. Mark 4:39

GOD HAS A PLAN.

"I know the plans I have for you," declares the LORD, "plans to prosper you, plans to give you hope and a future." Jeremiah 29:11

78

6 VITAL WAYS GOD ANSWERS YOU

YOU SAY:

1 "I'm exhausted."

2 "I am unloved."

3 "I don't know what to do."

4 "I'm afraid."

5 "I can't handle this anymore."

6 "I am worthless."

GOD SAYS:

"Wait on Me. I will renew your strength."
ISAIAH 40:31

"I have loved you with an everlasting love." JEREMIAH 31:3

"I will direct your path." PROVERBS 3:6

"Don't be afraid. I am with you.
I will give you strength." ISAIAH 41:10

"Give your burdens to Me. I will take care of it." PSALM 55:22

"I have chosen you to be My own special treasure." DEUTERONOMY 7:6

79

4 *Quotes* TO GIVE YOU STRENGTH

"GOD'S WORK DONE IN GOD'S WAY will never lack God's *supply*."

Hudson Tayl

"BE FAITHFUL in small things because it is in THEM *that you* STRENGTH LIES."

Mother Teresa

"GOD *loves* EACH OF US as if there were ONLY ONE *of us.*"

St. Augustine

"God never said THAT THE *journey* would be easy, BUT HE DID SAY THAT THE *arrival* would be WORTHWHILE."

Max Lucado

WRITE DOWN 8 THINGS THAT
INSPIRE YOU
TO BE A
better parent

1.
_____
_____
_____

2.
_____
_____
_____

3.
_____
_____
_____

4.
_____
_____

THE **LORD**
has done *great*
THINGS FOR US
& we are **filled** with *joy.*
Psalm 126:3

5. _____
_____
_____

6. _____
_____
_____

7. _____
_____
_____

8. _____
_____
_____

81

6 Things grateful
Moms DO
EVERY DAY

♡ Practice gratitude with a gratitude journal.

♡ Spend some time enjoying the beauty of God's creation.

♡ Eat a deliciously healthy breakfast.

♡ Listen to really good music.

♡ Get enough sleep.

♡ Hydrate with some
fruit-infused water.

A cheerful heart ✓ is good
medicine.

Proverbs 17:22

4 NAMES GOD has for you

MY CHILD

See how very much our Father loves us, for He calls us His children, and that is what we are!

1 John 3:1

BELOVED

As the elect of God, holy and beloved, put on tender mercies, kindness, humility, meekness, long-suffering ...

Colossians 3:12

CO-HEIR WITH CHRIST

Since we are His children, we are
His heirs. In fact, together with Christ
we are heirs of God's glory.

Romans 8:17

AMBASSADOR

We are Christ's ambassadors;
God is making His appeal through us.

2 Corinthians 5:20

CHOOSE A *good* *reputation* OVER GREAT RICHES;

LIST 10 THINGS YOU WANT TO BE REMEMBERED FOR:

[1]

[2]

[3]

[4]

[5]

BEING HELD IN
high esteem
IS *better* THAN
SILVER OR GOLD.
Proverbs 22:1

[6]

[7]

[8]

[q]

[l0]

7 BIBLE *Verses* FOR BEING A MORE PATIENT PARENT

One So let's not get tired of doing what is good. At just the right time we will reap a harvest of blessing if we don't give up. Galatians 6:9

Two The Holy Spirit produces this kind of fruit in our lives: love, joy, peace, patience ... Galatians 5:22

Three Better to be patient than powerful. Proverbs 16:32

Four You, too, must be patient. Take courage, for the coming of the Lord is near. James 5:8

Five

Be still before the L\ord and wait patiently for Him. Psalm 37:7

Six

Live a life worthy of the calling you have received. Be completely humble and gentle; be patient, bearing with one another in love. Ephesians 4:1-2

Seven The patient in spirit is better than the proud in spirit. Ecclesiastes 7:8

85

FRIENDS COME
& FRIENDS GO,
but a
TRUE FRIEND
sticks by you like
family.

PROVERBS 18:24

7 WAYS
TO BE A *good*
FRIEND

1. Listen when your friend speaks without interrupting her.

2. Ask her how she is and listen with interest to her response.

3. Encourage and support her in her new endeavors.

4. Help her whenever you can in whichever way she needs.

5. Always be honest and never talk behind her back.

6. Be trustworthy with her secrets.

7. Pray for her.

A GODLY *Mom* KNOWS ...

EVERY CHILD IS *important*

WHEN TO BE *protective*

WHEN TO
let go

HOW TO
trust God

GOD DOES NOT
BLESS PERFECT
PARENTING,

He blesses

HUMBLE PARENTING.

177

5 RANDOM ACTS OF *love*

1 Buy a cup of coffee for a friend.

2 Phone your parents or grandparents just to say hi.

3 Leave your colleague a note of encouragement.

4 Volunteer at your church or an animal rescue center.

5 Make a little extra food for lunch and share it with someone in need.

Do everything in love.

1 Corinthians 16:14

LIST 10
THINGS THAT DESCRIBE YOU AS
A MOM

1

2

3

4

5

6
7
8
9
10

We are
God's masterpiece.

EPHESIANS 2:10

MOTHERS WHO PERSEVERE DON'T ...

- expect fast results

- stop believing in themselves

- dwell on their mistakes

- focus on the past

- resist change

- fear what might happen

- assume their problems are unique

- see failure as a sign to stop

- feel sorry for themselves

- complain more than they work

- stop trusting in God

BE STRONG
AND DO NOT
GIVE UP,
FOR YOUR *work*
WILL BE
REWARDED.

2 CHRONICLES 15:7

90

6 Tips
TO TEACH

TREAT OTHERS THE WAY YOU WANT TO BE TREATED.

ALWAYS BE KIND TO EVERYONE.

LISTEN TO WHAT OTHERS HAVE TO SAY.

DON'T BE JEALOUS OR PROUD, BUT BE HUMBLE AND CONSIDER OTHERS MORE IMPORTANT THAN YOURSELVES.

PHILIPPIANS 2:3

YOUR Children
RESPECT

DON'T MAKE EXCUSES, MAKE A PLAN.

DON'T MAKE PROMISES YOU CANNOT KEEP.

BE OPEN TO CHANGE AND NEW IDEAS.

4 WAYS TO MAKE SOMEONE'S *Day*

1 Make someone smile or laugh so hard they start to cry.

2 Write someone a thank-you note to let them know how grateful you are to have them in your life.

3 Tell someone you love them.

4 Surprise someone special to you with a small gift.

Give
THANKS
TO THE LORD
FOR HE IS GOOD!
HIS FAITHFUL LOVE
ENDURES
forever.
PSALM 136:1

92

5 HOPE-FILLED PROMISES TO HOLD ON TO

1. The LORD is good to those whose hope is in Him, to the one who seeks Him.

   Lamentations 3:25

2. Let us hold unswervingly to the hope we profess, for He who promised is faithful.

   Hebrews 10:23

3. Hope will not lead to disappointment. For we know how dearly God loves us.

   Romans 5:5

4. Be of good courage, and He
   shall strengthen your heart,
   all you who hope in the LORD.

   Psalm 31:24

5. We put our hope in the LORD.
   He is our help and our shield.

   Psalm 33:20

6 PIECES OF *Armor*

1 BELT OF TRUTH

2 BREASTPLATE OF RIGHTEOUSNESS

3 SHOES OF THE GOSPEL OF PEACE

FOR A WARRIOR MOM

SHIELD OF FAITH

4

HELMET OF SALVATION

5

SWORD OF THE SPIRIT

6

Put on every piece of God's armor so you will be able to resist the enemy.

Ephesians 6:13

4 THINGS JESUS Promises you

1. AN ABUNDANT LIFE.

"I have come that they may have life, and have it to the full." John 10:10

2. ETERNAL LIFE.

"Everyone who lives in Me and believes in Me will never ever die." John 11:26

3. AN ANSWER TO YOUR PRAYERS.

"If you believe, you will receive whatever you ask for in prayer." Matthew 21:22

4. YOU WILL NEVER BE ALONE.

"I will not leave you as orphans; I will come to you." John 14:18

Consider Jesus.
Soak in the shadow
of Jesus. Saturate your
soul with the ways of
Jesus. Watch Him.
Listen to Him.
Stand in awe of Him.
Let Him overwhelm you
with the way He is.

John Piper

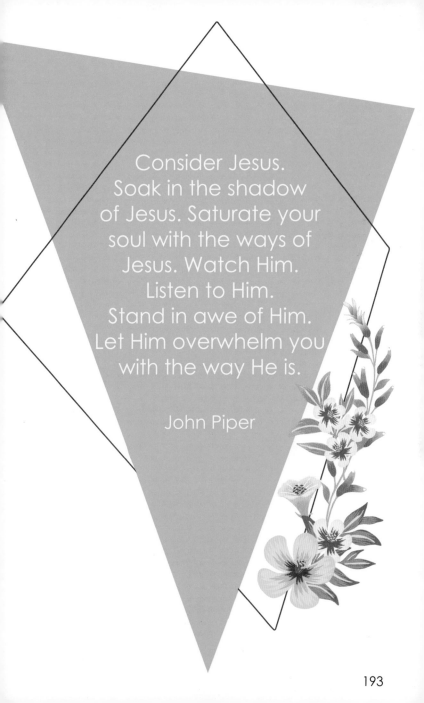

95

8 REASONS
WHY YOU CAN BE
confident

> BLESSED
> ARE THOSE WHO
> TRUST IN THE LORD
> AND HAVE MADE THE
> LORD THEIR HOPE
> AND CONFIDENCE.
>
> JEREMIAH 17:7

God has made you fearless and strong.

Failures are opportunities to grow.

Nothing is impossible as long as you believe in God.

Make a difference by showing up
and giving it your all.

Become a better version of yourself.

You are blessed beyond measure.

Challenges are just another learning
experience.

You have been created for a marvelous purpose.

96

6 Questions to ask

BEFORE MAKING
IMPORTANT DECISIONS

SEEK *His will* IN ALL YOU DO, AND HE WILL SHOW YOU *which path* TO TAKE.

PROVERBS 3:6

1. DOES THIS FIT WITH MY SKILLS?

2. WHAT DO THE PEOPLE I TRUST MOST SAY ABOUT IT?

3. DOES THIS LINE UP WITH SCRIPTURE AND DO I UNDERSTAND GOD'S PURPOSE FOR ME?

4. DO I FEEL AN INNER TUG OR "LEADING" FROM GOD TO DO IT?

5. IF I SAY YES, WHAT WILL IT MEAN SAYING NO TO?

6. WHEN I LOOK BACK IN TEN YEARS, WILL THIS BE A STORY I WANT TO SHARE?

97

6 Things EVERY GODLY MOM DOES

1. Invests in her children's spiritual growth.

2. Stays plugged in to God.

3. Reaches out to others for help.

4. Feeds herself with the Word.

5. Uses her example to point her children to Jesus.

6. Prays for and with her kids.

Always be *joyful,*

NEVER STOP
PRAYING.
Be thankful
IN ALL
CIRCUMSTANCES.

1 Thessalonians 5:16-18

7 TRUTHS TO REMEMBER
WHEN YOU PRAY

I AM
LOVED.
JOHN 3:16

GOD'S WORD
IS A LAMP
TO MY FEET.
PSALM 119:105

1.

3.

2.

4.

I AM
FORGIVEN.
MATTHEW 26:27-28

THE LORD
IS MY HELP
PSALM 121

I AM CHOSEN.

1 PETER 2:9

**GOD IS
WORKING IT
ALL OUT
FOR MY GOOD.**

ROMANS 8:28

5.

7.

6.

**HE WHO IS IN ME
IS GREATER THAN HE WHO
IS IN THE WORLD.**

1 JOHN 4:4

4 Inspiring Quotes
from Women in the Bible

Rebekah

"I will go."

Genesis 24:58

Leah

"This time
I will praise
the LORD."

Genesis 29:35

Ruth

"Your people shall be my people, and your God, my God."

Ruth 1:16

Mary

"Behold, I am the servant of the Lord ..."

Luke 1:38

5 OF GOD'S DESIRES FOR *Moms*

Gentleness
A humble attitude softened by
knowledge of God's grace.

Quietness
Confidence in the Lord that leads
to wise speech and kind action.

Hope
Trust in Christ's sovereignty
and Second Coming that gives joy.

Faithfulness
Determination to do good
and obey God in love.

Fearlessness
Having courage in light of God's
steadfast promises.

YOU SHOULD

clothe

YOURSELVES INSTEAD

with the

BEAUTY

THAT COMES FROM WITHIN ...

which is so

PRECIOUS

— TO GOD —

1 Peter 3:4

101

9 CHARACTERISTICS
of a Godly Mom

If you have
a gift for showing
kindness to others,
do it gladly.

Romans 12:8

After God's
Own Heart

1. She raises her children according to His will

2. She is a servant

3. She is selfless

4. She teaches good things

5. She loves her husband and children

6. She turns a house into a home

7. She is kind

8. She is thankful

9. She loves God above all.

Lord,
MAY I ALWAYS
BE A PERSON FILLED WITH  *gratitude*
IN MY HEART
for all things.
Thank **YOU**
FOR OPENING MY EYES
TO THE MANY WAYS I CAN
GIVE THANKS.
Amen